Let's Make Music

Jessica Baron

Rosen **REAL** **READERS**

Rosen Classroom Books and Materials
New York

It is fun to listen to music. Music can make you feel good.

It is fun to make music. Everyone can do it!

You can clap and make music
with your hands.

You can snap and make music with your fingers.

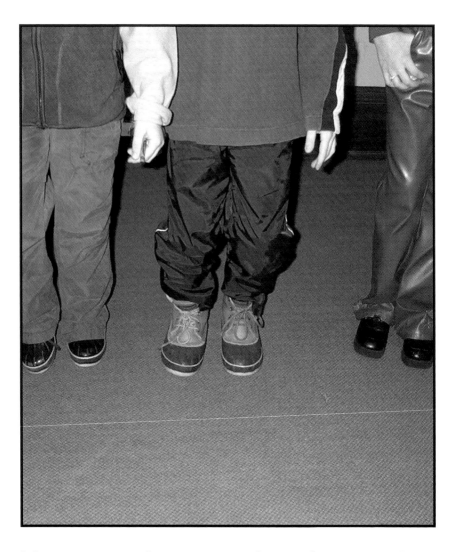

You can stomp and make music
with your feet.

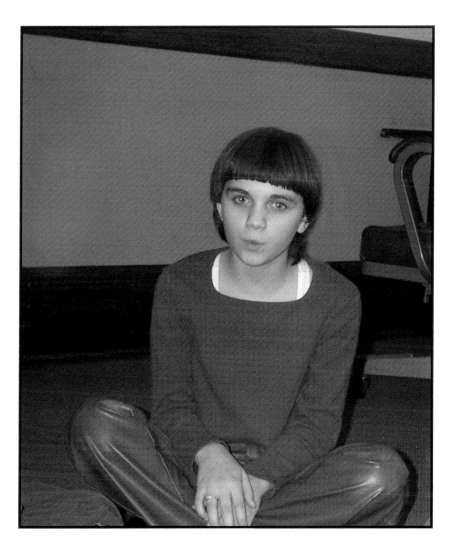

You can whistle and make music with your lips.

You can sing and make music with your voice. It is fun to sing with your friends.

You can make music with objects. You can play the recorder.

You can make music by yourself.

You can make music with your friends. Have fun!

Words To Know

clap

recorder

snap

stomp

whistle